YEARS AND YEARS

DO YOU REMEMBER THIS?

1959

PEOPLE, MUSIC, FILMS EVENTS IN THE UK FROM THE YEAR YOU WERE BORN!

UK VERSION

The story, all names, characters, and incidents portrayed in this production are fictitious. No identification with actual persons (living or deceased), places, buildings, and products is intended or should be inferred.

"Memories and thoughts age, just as people do. But certain thoughts can never age, and certain memories can never fade."

(Haruki Murakami)

CONTENTS

A little bit of time travel - did we really do that then - and what do we do now that would have been like science fiction then?

YEAR BY YEAR: 1959

YEARS AND YEARS: 1959

1959
CALENDAR

1959

January						
Mon		5	12	19	26	
Tue		6	13	20	27	
Wed		7	14	21	28	
Thu	1	8	15	22	29	
Fri	2	9	16	23	30	
Sat	3	10	17	24	31	
Sun	4	11	18	25		

February					
Mon		2	9	16	23
Tue		3	10	17	24
Wed		4	11	18	25
Thu		5	12	19	26
Fri		6	13	20	27
Sat		7	14	21	28
Sun	1	8	15	22	

March						
Mon		2	9	16	23	30
Tue		3	10	17	24	31
Wed		4	11	18	25	
Thu		5	12	19	26	
Fri		6	13	20	27	
Sat		7	14	21	28	
Sun	1	8	15	22	29	

April					
Mon		6	13	20	27
Tue		7	14	21	28
Wed	1	8	15	22	29
Thu	2	9	16	23	30
Fri	3	10	17	24	
Sat	4	11	18	25	
Sun	5	12	19	26	

May					
Mon		4	11	18	25
Tue		5	12	19	26
Wed		6	13	20	27
Thu		7	14	21	28
Fri	1	8	15	22	29
Sat	2	9	16	23	30
Sun	3	10	17	24	31

June					
Mon	1	8	15	22	29
Tue	2	9	16	23	30
Wed	3	10	17	24	
Thu	4	11	18	25	
Fri	5	12	19	26	
Sat	6	13	20	27	
Sun	7	14	21	28	

July					
Mon		6	13	20	27
Tue		7	14	21	28
Wed	1	8	15	22	29
Thu	2	9	16	23	30
Fri	3	10	17	24	31
Sat	4	11	18	25	
Sun	5	12	19	26	

August						
Mon		3	10	17	24	31
Tue		4	11	18	25	
Wed		5	12	19	26	
Thu		6	13	20	27	
Fri		7	14	21	28	
Sat	1	8	15	22	29	
Sun	2	9	16	23	30	

September					
Mon		7	14	21	28
Tue	1	8	15	22	29
Wed	2	9	16	23	30
Thu	3	10	17	24	
Fri	4	11	18	25	
Sat	5	12	19	26	
Sun	6	13	20	27	

October					
Mon		5	12	19	26
Tue		6	13	20	27
Wed		7	14	21	28
Thu	1	8	15	22	29
Fri	2	9	16	23	30
Sat	3	10	17	24	31
Sun	4	11	18	25	

November						
Mon		2	9	16	23	30
Tue		3	10	17	24	
Wed		4	11	18	25	
Thu		5	12	19	26	
Fri		6	13	20	27	
Sat		7	14	21	28	
Sun	1	8	15	22	29	

December					
Mon		7	14	21	28
Tue	1	8	15	22	29
Wed	2	9	16	23	30
Thu	3	10	17	24	31
Fri	4	11	18	25	
Sat	5	12	19	26	
Sun	6	13	20	27	

ON WHAT DAY OF THE WEEK WERE *YOU* BORN?

A Pivotal Year: A Review of Events in the United Kingdom in 1959

The year 1959 emerged as a crucial juncture in the history of the United Kingdom, marking a confluence of political, social, and cultural transformations that would shape the nation's trajectory. This extensive review aims to delve into the significant events that unfolded during this pivotal year, offering a nuanced perspective on the political landscape, social dynamics, and cultural shifts that defined the era.

Political Landscape:

1. General Election of 1959:

The cornerstone of 1959's political landscape was undoubtedly the General Election held on October 8th. The Conservative Party, led by the seasoned politician Harold Macmillan, secured a resounding victory, consolidating its hold on the government. This election was more than a routine political event; it was a reflection of the prevailing sentiment in the country, with Macmillan's campaign capitalizing on the theme of affluence and stability. The famous slogan, "You've never had it so good," became emblematic of an era defined by economic prosperity.

Macmillan's victory in 1959 was a testament to the Conservative government's policies promoting growth and development. The post-war recovery was evident, and the election campaign successfully highlighted the contrast between the austerity of the immediate post-war years and the economic prosperity that had become a hallmark of the late 1950s.

2. Macmillan's Conservative Government:

With his re-election, Prime Minister Harold Macmillan steered the Conservative government towards a continuation of policies promoting economic growth and stability. The administration's emphasis on housing and consumerism aimed to create a "property-owning democracy," wherein a larger segment of the population could aspire to own their homes. Macmillan's leadership style and his government's focus on a vision of affluence contributed to a sense of optimism and confidence in the nation's future.

The aftermath of the Suez Crisis in 1956 continued to influence Macmillan's foreign policy decisions. The declining significance of imperial power and the necessity for international cooperation became central themes, shaping the UK's global standing and diplomatic endeavors.

Social Dynamics:

1. Changing Social Fabric:

Beyond the political arena, the late 1950s witnessed a profound shift in the social fabric of the United Kingdom. Traditional values were undergoing a metamorphosis, giving rise to a more liberal and permissive culture. This cultural transformation was visible in various facets of society, including the arts, media, and societal norms. The decade marked the beginning of a departure from the rigid social structures that had defined the early post-war years.

2. Television and Popular Culture:

Television emerged as a powerful force shaping public opinion and cultural trends. The mid-1950s saw the rise of commercial television, and its impact continued to reverberate in 1959. Iconic shows such as "Hancock's Half Hour" and "Emergency – Ward 10" not only entertained but also reflected and influenced societal norms. The cultural influence of television was a precursor to the media-driven society that would fully blossom in the subsequent decades.

The portrayal of everyday life on television contributed to a sense of shared experiences and a growing national identity. It played a crucial role in shaping fashion, music preferences, and consumer behaviour, setting the stage for a more interconnected and culturally cohesive society.

3. Youth Culture and the Rise of the Teenager:

One of the most significant social phenomena of 1959 was the emergence of a distinct youth culture. The term "teenager" gained prominence, signifying a demographic with its own unique tastes, preferences, and aspirations. This demographic shift was propelled by the rise of rock 'n' roll music, with artists like Elvis Presley and Buddy Holly becoming cultural icons. The rebellious spirit of the youth culture challenged established norms, paving the way for a more individualistic and expressive generation.

The newfound freedom and identity of teenagers marked a departure from the conformist ideals of the previous generation. The cultural shift in 1959 laid the groundwork for the social revolutions of the 1960s, as the youth culture continued to evolve and shape the trajectory of British society.

Cultural Shifts:

1. Literary Landscape:

The literary landscape of 1959 was marked by the publication of influential works that resonated with the evolving spirit of the times. Ian Fleming's "Goldfinger," part of the James Bond series, captured the imagination of readers with its suave protagonist and espionage-laden plot. The Bond series, which gained widespread popularity, reflected the fascination with spy fiction that characterized the Cold War era.

Doris Lessing, an influential author and Nobel laureate, published "The Four-Gated City" in 1959. This work delved into themes of dystopia and societal collapse, providing a thought-provoking commentary on the state of the world. Lessing's exploration of existential questions and the human condition resonated with readers and critics alike, contributing to the literary discourse of the time.

2. Music and the British Invasion:

The musical landscape of 1959 laid the foundation for the British Invasion that would define the 1960s. While rock 'n' roll continued to dominate, the emergence of British pop music was evident in the work of artists like Cliff Richard and The Shadows. These artists, influenced by American rock 'n' roll but adding their own distinct flavor, paved the way for the global influence of British music in the coming decade.

The late 1950s also witnessed the establishment of influential music labels, contributing to the growth of the recording industry. This period marked the transition from the dominance of singles to the emergence of the album as a cohesive artistic expression. The groundwork laid in 1959 set the stage for the transformative musical experiences of the 1960s, with bands like The Beatles revolutionizing the industry.

3. Art and Fashion:

The art world in 1959 reflected a dynamic interplay between traditional and modernist influences. Established artists like Francis Bacon continued to make significant contributions to the art scene, challenging conventional artistic norms. The emergence of a new generation of artists, often associated with the "Young British Artists" (YBAs) movement in the subsequent decades, signaled a departure from traditional artistic conventions.

The world of fashion also underwent notable transformations in 1959. The post-war austerity that had characterized previous years began to wane, and a newfound sense of optimism was reflected in clothing styles. The late 1950s set the stage for the iconic fashion trends of the 1960s, with the influence of designers like Mary Quant and the introduction of the miniskirt becoming emblematic of the changing times.

As the nation navigated the complexities of post-war recovery, global realignments, and the challenges of a rapidly evolving society, 1959 laid the groundwork for the cultural and social revolutions that would define the following decade. The seeds of the swinging sixties were sown in the political, social, and cultural shifts of 1959, setting the stage for a period of unprecedented change and innovation. In essence, the events of 1959 shaped the trajectory of the United Kingdom, leaving an indelible mark on its history and influencing the course of subsequent decades.

Economic Landscape:

1. Post-War Economic Recovery:

The economic landscape of 1959 was deeply influenced by the ongoing process of post-war recovery. The post-war years had seen the UK rebuilding its economy, and by 1959, the nation was experiencing a period of sustained growth. This economic prosperity played a pivotal role in shaping the political discourse and contributed to the sense of optimism prevalent in the era.

2. Consumerism and the Affluent Society:

A noteworthy feature of the late 1950s was the rise of consumerism. The increased availability of goods and the growing purchasing power of the middle class contributed to the emergence of what was often referred to as the "affluent society." The consumer boom was not only a result of economic growth but also a catalyst for societal changes. The idea that individuals could aspire to a higher standard of living became a driving force, influencing not only political rhetoric but also social aspirations.

3. Technological Advances:

The late 1950s saw significant strides in technological innovation. This period marked the beginning of the space race, with the launch of the Luna 1 spacecraft by the Soviet Union in 1959. The space race had profound implications for global geopolitics, but it also symbolized a broader embrace of scientific progress and technological advancement. These developments not only impacted industry and defence but also contributed to a sense of modernity and optimism about the future.

International Relations:

1. Cold War Dynamics:

The geopolitical landscape of 1959 was dominated by the Cold War between the United States and the Soviet Union. The United Kingdom, as a key player in global affairs, navigated the complexities of this ideological and geopolitical conflict. The Suez Crisis of 1956 had highlighted the changing dynamics of global power, and by 1959, the UK was adjusting its foreign policy to align with the realities of the Cold War.

2. Decolonization and the End of Empire:

The process of decolonization, which had been underway since the end of World War II, continued to shape the UK's international relations in 1959. Former colonies in Africa and Asia were gaining independence, marking the end of the British Empire. This process had profound implications for the UK's global influence and required a reassessment of diplomatic and economic priorities.

3. European Integration:

The late 1950s saw the initial steps toward European integration. The Treaty of Rome, signed in 1957, established the European Economic Community (EEC), laying the groundwork for what would later become the European Union. While the UK did not initially join the EEC, these developments signalled a shift in the geopolitical landscape, emphasizing the importance of regional cooperation and economic integration.

Social Movements and Civil Rights:

1. Windrush Generation and Immigration:

The arrival of the Windrush Generation in the late 1940s and early 1950s had a profound impact on the social fabric of the UK. In 1959, the descendants of Caribbean immigrants were becoming an integral part of British society. The cultural exchange and contributions of the Windrush Generation added diversity to the nation and set the stage for the multicultural identity that would define modern Britain.

2. Civil Rights Movement:

While the Civil Rights Movement in the United States gained international attention, its ideals resonated with individuals and groups in the UK. The late 1950s saw the beginnings of a British civil rights movement, with a focus on combating racial discrimination and advocating for equal rights. The struggles faced by minority communities during this period laid the groundwork for later advancements in civil rights and social justice.

Education and Intellectual Discourse:

1. Educational Reforms:

The late 1950s witnessed a series of educational reforms aimed at expanding access to education. The Education Act of 1959, for example, sought to address issues of overcrowded schools and inadequate facilities. These reforms were part of a broader effort to democratize education and provide equal opportunities for all segments of society.

2. Intellectual Debates:

The intellectual landscape of 1959 was marked by vibrant debates on issues ranging from nuclear disarmament to the role of the state in the economy. Thinkers and academics engaged in discussions that shaped public discourse and influenced policy decisions. The intellectual ferment of the time reflected a society grappling with the implications of technological advancements, the complexities of the Cold War, and the challenges of a changing world.

In conclusion, the events of 1959 in the United Kingdom were multifaceted, encompassing not only political and cultural shifts but also economic, international, and social developments. The optimism of the era, fueled by economic prosperity and cultural dynamism, coexisted with the challenges posed by geopolitical tensions, decolonization, and social inequality. This comprehensive review aims to capture the richness and complexity of a pivotal year that laid the groundwork for the transformative decade that followed.

Conclusion:

In retrospect, the year 1959 in the United Kingdom emerged as a crucible of change, capturing the essence of a nation in the midst of a profound transformation. The political landscape, characterized by the re-election of the Conservative government under Harold Macmillan, reflected a desire for continuity and stability. Socially and culturally, the late 1950s witnessed a departure from traditional norms, paving the way for the dynamic and influential era of the 1960s.

POPULAR CULTURE

1959 Popular Culture

- The US Grammy Music Awards Started

- The last musical from Rodgers and Hammerstein "The Sound of Music" opens on Broadway

- The chartered plane transporting musicians Buddy Holly, Richie Valens, and the Big Bopper goes down in an Iowa snowstorm, killing all four occupants on board. The tragedy is later termed "The Day the Music Died," popularized in Don McLean's song, "American Pie."

- The Film Ben-Hur premieres in New York City

Popular Films

- Ben-Hur

- Some Like It Hot

- Anatomy of a Murder

- North by Northwest

- Sleeping Beauty

Popular TV

- Bonanza premieres on NBC, the first weekly television series broadcast completely in colour

- Juke Box Jury premieres on BBC Television

- Dixon of Dock Green

- The Huckleberry Hound Show

Popular Singers

- Elvis Presley

- Paul Anka

- The Platters

- Doris Day

- Frank Sinatra

- Connie Francis

- Jim Reeves

- Cliff Richard

- Ella Fitzgerald

Billie Holiday

1959 saw the loss of musical icon Billie Holiday, one of the greatest jazz singers in history. She is remembered for having one of the most outstanding jazz voices in the music industry, managing to have a fascinating and busy career before sadly facing addiction struggles.

After a troubling childhood, Billie Holiday found peace in music, frequently listening to Louis Armstrong and Bessie Smith. Her career took off when she began singing in local clubs during the 1930s. A performance in a Harlem jazz club led her to be recognised by a producer, and she soon began to record. Her life became filled with popular songs and tours, including a film appearance in Symphony in Black.

In 1945, Holiday's addiction struggles began to surface when she started using drugs with her current boyfriend and faced conviction charges for the possession of narcotics. Her final performance was on May 25, 1959, soon before she was admitted to hospital for heart and liver problems. From alcohol and drug-related problems, Holiday passed away on July 17, 1959.

Her funeral was attended by more than 3,000 people who wished to say their goodbyes, revealing the true impact her music and performances had on the public. Many well-known jazz faces also made an appearance at the funeral, including Gene Krupa and Buddy Rogers. She was posthumously inducted into the Rock and Roll Hall of Fame in 2000, and she also received career achievement awards at the 29th annual Grammy Awards.

The Twilight Zone

The iconic science fiction television series "The Twilight Zone" airs for the first time on October 2nd, on the CBS television network. The Twilight Zone was created and hosted by the talented screenwriter Rod Serling. The Twilight Zone still ranks as one of the most unique and best-written television shows in TV history. It ran for five seasons until 1964 and had a total of 156 episodes. Of those 156 episodes, 92 were written by Serling himself, and many of them contain some of the most memorable television moments. The show consisted of sci-fi and supernatural mysteries in an anthology setting and featured many then-unknown actors who would later become famous, like Ron Howard, Dennis Hopper, Robert Redford and William Shatner.

BEST-SELLING RECORDS OF 1959

HOW MANY OF THESE FAMOUS SINGERS CAN YOU IDENTIFY?

1959 TOP 20 MUSIC CHARTS

1. It's Only Make Believe Conway Twitty NUMBER ONE FOR 5 WEEKS

2. January 23rd 1959 The Day the Rains Came Jane Morgan NUMBER ONE FOR 1 WEEK

3. January 30th 1959 One Night / I Got Stung Elvis Presley NUMBER ONE FOR 3 WEEKS

4. February 20th 1959 As I Love You Shirley Bassey NUMBER ONE FOR 4 WEEKS

5. March 20th 1959 Smoke Gets in Your Eyes The Platters NUMBER ONE FOR 1 WEEK

6. March 27th 1959 Side Saddle Russ Conway NUMBER ONE FOR 4 WEEKS

7. April 24th 1959 It Doesn't Matter Anymore Buddy Holly NUMBER ONE FOR 3 WEEKS

8. May 15th 1959 A Fool Such as I Elvis Presley NUMBER ONE FOR 5 WEEKS

9. June 19th 1959 Roulette Russ Conway NUMBER ONE FOR 2 WEEKS

10. July 3rd 1959 Dream Lover Bobby Darin NUMBER ONE FOR 4 WEEKS

11. July 31st 1959 Living Doll Cliff Richard and The Drifters NUMBER ONE FOR 6 WEEKS

12. September 11th 1959 Only Sixteen Craig Douglas NUMBER ONE FOR 4 WEEKS

13. October 9th 1959 Here Comes Summer Jerry Keller NUMBER ONE FOR 1 WEEK

14. October 16th 1959 Mack the Knife Bobby Darin NUMBER ONE FOR 2 WEEKS

15. October 30th 1959 Travellin' Light Cliff Richard and The Shadows NUMBER ONE FOR 5 WEEKS

16. December 4th 1959 What Do You Want? Adam Faith NUMBER ONE FOR 2 WEEKS

17. December 18th 1959 What Do You Want? / What Do You Want to Make Those Eyes at Me For? (joint Number One)

Adam Faith/ Emile Ford and The Checkmates (joint Number One) NUMBER ONE FOR 1 WEEK

18. December 25th 1959 What Do You Want to Make Those Eyes at Me For? Emile Ford and The Checkmates NUMBER ONE FOR 5 WEEKS

BEST SELLER OF THE YEAR: LIVING DOLL

AND IN THE USA?

The Christmas Song - The Chipmunks & David Seville (2 weeks)

Smoke Gets In Your Eyes - The Platters (3 weeks)

Stagger Lee - Lloyd Price (4 weeks)

Venus - Frankie Avalon (5 weeks)

Come Softly To Me - The Fleetwoods (4 weeks)

The Happy Organ - Dave "Baby" Cortez (1 week)

Kansas City - Wilbert Harrison (2 weeks)

The Battle of New Orleans - Johnny Horton (6 weeks)

Lonely Boy - Paul Anka (4 weeks)

A Big Hunk O' Love - Elvis Presley (2 weeks)

The Three Bells - The Browns (4 weeks)

Sleepwalk - Santo & Johnny (2 weeks)

Mack The Knife - Bobby Darin (9 weeks)

Mr. Blue - The Fleetwoods (1 week)

Heartaches By The Number - Guy Mitchell (2 weeks)

Why - Frankie Avalon (1 week)

BEST SELLER OF THE YEAR The Battle of New Orleans - Johnny Horton

HE ENTERTAINMENT EXPERIENCE OF A LIFETIME!
BEST-GROSSING MOVIES OF 1959
HOW MANY OF THESE FAMOUS FILMS DID YOU WATCH?

 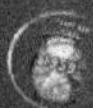

TOP MOVIES OF 1959

1. North by Northwest 1959, 136 min.

Alfred Hitchcock • Starring: Cary Grant, Eva Marie Saint, James Mason

Chase Movie • Mystery • Romance

2. Some Like It Hot 1959, 120 min.

Billy Wilder • Starring: Marilyn Monroe, Tony Curtis, Jack Lemmon

Comedy of Errors • Comedy • Cross-Dressing / Gender-Bending

3. Ben-Hur 1959, 212 min.

William Wyler • Starring: Charlton Heston, Jack Hawkins, Haya Harareet

4. House on Haunted Hill 1959, 75 min.

William Castle • Starring: Vincent Price, Carol Ohmart, Richard Long

5. The Hound of the Baskervilles 1959, 87 min.

Terence Fisher • Starring: David Oxley, Christopher Lee, Marla Landi

Based-on-20th-Century-Literature • Crime • Detective Film

6. Suddenly, Last Summer 1959, 114 min.

Joseph L. Mankiewicz • Starring: Elizabeth Taylor, Katharine Hepburn, Montgomery Clift

Drama • Medical Drama • Melodrama

7. Journey to the Center of the Earth 1959, 132 min.

Henry Levin • Starring: Pat Boone, James Mason, Arlene Dahl

Adventure • Based-on-19th-Century-Literature • Costume Adventure

8. The Mummy 1959, 88 min.

Terence Fisher • Starring: Peter Cushing, Christopher Lee, Yvonne Furneaux

Costume Horror • Horror • Monster Film

9. The Diary of Anne Frank 1959, 180 min.

George Stevens • Starring: Millie Perkins, Joseph Schildkraut, Shelley Winters

Based-on-a-True-Story • Biopic • Drama

10. Room at the Top 1959, 115 min.

Jack Clayton • Starring: Simone Signoret, Heather Sears, Donald Houston

British New Wave • Drama • Melodrama

11. The Mouse That Roared 1959, 83 min.

Jack Arnold • Starring: Peter Sellers, Jean Seberg, William Hartnell

Comedy • Satire

12. Plan 9 from Outer Space 1959, 79 min.

Edward D. Wood Jr. • Starring: Mona McKinnon, Criswell, Bela Lugosi

13. The 39 Steps 1959, 93 min.

Ralph Thomas • Starring: Kenneth More, Taina Elg, Brenda de Banzie

Based-on-20th-Century-Literature • Chase Movie • Drama

14. I'm All Right Jack 1959, 100 min.

John Boulting • Starring: Ian Carmichael, Terry-Thomas, Peter Sellers

Comedy • Satire • Workplace Comedy

15. Return of the Fly 1959, 80 min.

Edward Bernds • Starring: Vincent Price, Brett Halsey, John Sutton

Body Horror • Horror • Monster Film

16. Carry On Nurse 1959, 86 min.

Gerald Thomas • Starring: Kenneth Connor, Charles Hawtrey, Kenneth Williams

Comedy • Farce • Parody/Spoof

17. Carry On Teacher 1959, 86 min.

Gerald Thomas • Starring: Ted Ray, Kenneth Connor, Kenneth Williams

Comedy • Farce • Parody/Spoof

18. Horrors of the Black Museum 1959, 95 min.

Arthur Crabtree • Starring: Michael Gough, June Cunningham, Graham Curnow

Horror • Psychological Horror • Psychological Thriller

19. The Navy Lark 1959, 82 min.

Gordon Parry • Starring: Cecil Parker, Ronald Shiner, Leslie Phillips

Comedy • Military Comedy

20. Sleeping beauty

Top 10 Highest grossing Movies 1959

1 Ben-Hur Nov 18, 1959 MGM Adventure $73,000,000

2 The Shaggy Dog Mar 19, 1959 $29,000,000

3 Some Like it Hot Mar 29, 1959 Romantic Comedy $25,000,000

4 Operation Petticoat Dec 5, 1959 Romantic Comedy $23,300,000

5 Pillow Talk Jan 1, 1959 Romantic Comedy $18,750,000

6 Imitation of Life Apr 30, 1959 Drama $14,000,000

7 North by Northwest Jan 1, 1959 Thriller/Suspense $13,275,000

8 The Nun's Story Jul 18, 1959 Drama $12,800,000

9 A Hole in the Head Jul 15, 1959 $11,000,000

10 Solomon and Sheba Jan 1, 1959

A FEW SNIPPETS OF TRIVIA ABOUT BEN-HUR

The chariot race required 15,000 extras on a set constructed on 18 acres of backlot at Cinecitta Studios outside Rome. Tour buses visited the set every hour. Eighteen chariots were built, with half being used for practice. The race took five weeks to film.

During the 18-day auction of MGM props, costumes and memorabilia that took place in May 1970 when new studio owner Kirk Kerkorian was liquidating the studio's assets, a Sacramento restaurateur paid $4,000 for a chariot used in the film. Three years later, during the energy crisis, he was arrested for driving the chariot on the highway.

Kirk Douglas was offered the role of Messala but turned it down, because he didn't want to play a "second-rate baddie". Douglas wanted to play Judah Ben-Hur, whose Jewishness appealed to him, but he was too old and Charlton Heston had already been cast. The experience motivated Douglas to develop his own epic, Spartacus (1960), which was partially designed to compete against this film.

The chariot race has a 263-to-1 cutting ratio (263 feet of film for every one foot used), probably the highest for any 65mm sequence ever filmed.

BREAK-DOWN OF THE YEAR BY MONTH

THE TOP TEN EVENTS OF THE YEAR

1. Fidel Castro came to power in Cuba after a Revolution

2. United States Vice President Richard Nixon and the Soviet Union's Premier Nikita Khrushchev engage in an impromptu debate

3. The Dalai Lama and tens of thousands of Tibetans flee to India after China Invades Tibet

4. Hawaii becomes the 50th state

5. NASA launches the Pioneer 4 spacecraft

6. United States - Canada - St. Lawrence Seaway is completed

7. The Antarctic Treaty is signed in Washington It was signed by twelve countries

8. The Luna 2 spacecraft crashes into the Moon

9. The Film Ben-Hur premieres

10. First Pictures Of Earth From Space Taken By Explorer 6

Incumbents: Monarch – Elizabeth II

Prime Minister – Harold Macmillan (Conservative)

Events by month

15 January – Tyne Tees Television, the ITV franchise for North East England, goes on the air.

22 January – Racing driver Mike Hawthorn is killed after his Jaguar 3.4-litre car collides with a tree on the A3 near Guildford.

29 January – Dense fog brings chaos to Britain.

19 February – First of the London and Zürich Agreements under which the UK agrees to grant independence to Cyprus.

23 February – Prime Minister Harold Macmillan holds talks with the Soviet leader Nikita Khrushchev on a visit to the USSR.

7 March – Independence movement leader Kanyama Chiume, wanted in the British territory of Nyasaland, flees to London and goes into hiding.

10 March – The comedy film Carlton-Browne of the F.O. is released.

30 March – 20,000 demonstrators attend a CND rally in Trafalgar Square.

1 April – The official name of the administrative county of Hampshire is changed from "County of Southampton" to "County of Hampshire".

2 April – United Dairies merges with Cow & Gate to form Unigate Dairies.

22 April – Ballerina Margot Fonteyn is released from prison in Panama following involvement in her husband's planned coup against the government of President Ernesto de la Guardia.

30 April – Icelandic gunboat fires on British trawlers in the first of the Cod Wars over fishing rights.

30 April – First Morris Mini-Minor off the production line, 8 May, ready for public launch in August.

2 May – The Chapelcross nuclear power station in Scotland opens.

Nottingham Forest beat Luton Town 2–1 in the FA Cup final at Wembley Stadium.

7 May – Scientist and novelist C. P. Snow delivers an influential Rede Lecture on The Two Cultures, concerning a perceived breakdown of communication between the sciences and humanities in the Senate House, University of Cambridge. It is subsequently published as The Two Cultures and the Scientific Revolution.

24 May – British Empire Day becomes Commonwealth Day.

28 May – The Mermaid Theatre opens in the City of London.

May – The first Ten Tors event is held on Dartmoor.

June – Import tariffs are lifted in the United Kingdom.

1 June – The first episode of Juke Box Jury airs on BBC Television, chaired by David Jacobs.

3 June – Singapore is granted self-governing status.

11 June – Christopher Cockerell's invention of the hovercraft is officially launched. On 25 July, the SR.N1 craft crosses the English Channel from Calais to Dover in just over 2 hours.

22 June – Harrods enters talks with Debenhams over a possible £34,000,000 merger.

23 June – Klaus Fuchs is released from Wakefield prison, having served over nine years for giving British nuclear secrets to the Soviet Union and moves to East Germany.

9 July – Wing Commander Michael Beetham flying a Royal Air Force Vickers Valiant, sets a record of 11 hours 27 minutes for a non-stop London–Cape Town flight.

10 July – Cliff Richard and The Drifters release a recording of the song "Living Doll", written by Lionel Bart.

28 July – UK postcodes are introduced for the first time, albeit as an experiment, in the city of Norwich.

29 July

The Mental Health Act became law, modernising the care of mental disorders.

The Obscene Publications Act became law.

The Legitimacy Act becomes law, permitting the legitimisation of a child, one of whose parents was married to a third person at the time of their birth, by the subsequent marriage of the parents.

4 August – Barclays became the first bank to install a computer.

24 August – House of Fraser wins the bidding war for Harrods in a £37,000,000 deal.

26 August – BMC launches the Mini to showrooms, a two-door, 10-foot-long car with an 848cc four-cylinder transverse engine and a top speed of 70mph, designed to carry the driver and three passengers and their luggage in comfort. The designer is Alec Issigonis who also designed the Morris Minor. It will remain in production until the year 2000 and be replaced with a BMW-made version a year later.

31 August – Harold Macmillan and US President Dwight Eisenhower make a joint television broadcast from Downing Street.

18 September – Auchengeich mining disaster: 47 miners die as the result of an underground fire at Auchengeich Colliery, Lanarkshire, Scotland.

7 October – Southend Pier is damaged in a fire.

8 October – The 1959 General Election is held, resulting in a record third successive Conservative victory. Harold Macmillan, running under the slogan "Life's better with the Conservatives, Don't let Labour ruin it", increased the Conservative majority in Parliament to 100 seats. The Labour Party contested their first (and only) General Election under the leadership of Hugh Gaitskell. Among the new Members of Parliament entering the Commons for the first time are future Prime Minister Margaret Thatcher, who will represent Finchley in North London for 33 years and future leader of the Liberal Party, Jeremy Thorpe.

12 October – A large-scale diamond robbery takes place in London.

21 October – Mau Mau leader Dedan Kimathi is arrested in Nyeri, Kenya.

30 October – Ronnie Scott's Jazz Club opens in the Soho district of London.

2 November – The first section of the M1 motorway is opened between Watford and Rugby. It is set to be extended over the next few years, southwards to Edgware and northwards to Leeds.

5 November – Philip John Noel-Baker wins the Nobel Peace Prize.

11 November – London Transport introduces the production AEC Routemaster double-decker bus into public service.

14 November – The nuclear Dounreay Fast Reactor in Scotland achieves criticality.

17 November – Prestwick and Renfrew Airport in Scotland become the first airports in the UK with duty-free shops.

20 November – Britain becomes a founder member of the European Free Trade Association.

December – Health enthusiast Dr Barbara Moore walks from Edinburgh to London.

6 December – Aberdeen trawler George Robb runs aground at Duncansby Head in Scotland in a severe gale with the loss of all 12 crew.

8 December – Broughty Ferry life-boat Mona capsizes on service to North Carr Lightship in Scotland, all eight life-boat crew are lost.

28 December – Associated-Rediffusion first airs the children's television series Ivor the Engine, made by Oliver Postgate and Peter Firmin's Smallfilms in stop motion animation using cardboard cut-outs.

Undated

London County Council completes the first portion of Alton Estate in Roehampton, southwest London, considered a model of post-war public housing.

"Aluminium War": concluding the first hostile takeover of a public company in the UK, Tube Investments (under its chairman Ivan Stedeford), allied with Reynolds Metals of the United States and advised by Siegmund Warburg of S. G. Warburg & Co., secure control of British Aluminium.

The iconic Bush TR82 transistor radio, by Ogle Design, is launched.

North of Scotland Hydro-Electric Board's Sloy-Awe Hydro-Electric Power Scheme becomes fully operational.

The Noise Abatement Society is established.

Car ownership in Britain now exceeds 30% of households.

Economic growth for the year is a very strong 7.2%, while the Retail Price Index shows a zero percentage change over the year.

Publications

Agatha Christie's novel Cat Among the Pigeons, featuring Hercule Poirot.

Ian Fleming's James Bond novel Goldfinger.

Colin MacInnes' novel Absolute Beginners.

Spike Milligan's collection Silly Verse for Kids.

Iona and Peter Opie's study The Lore and Language of Schoolchildren.

Mervyn Peake's novel Titus Alone completed the Gormenghast series.

Alan Sillitoe's story The Loneliness of the Long Distance Runner.

Keith Waterhouse's novel Billy Liar

DOCTOR ZHIVAGO, by Boris Pasternak.

LOLITA, by Vladimir Nabokov. (G.P. Putnam's Sons.) 2 19

AROUND THE WORLD WITH AUNTIE MAME, by Patrick Dennis.

ANATOMY OF A MURDER, by Robert Traver. (St. Martin's.) 9 50

THE KING MUST DIE, by Mary Renault. (Pantheon.) 13 23

THE BEST OF EVERYTHING, by Rona Jaffe. (Simon and Schuster.) 10 16

THE MOUNTAIN IS YOUNG, by Han Suyin. (Jonathan Cape.) 12 9

BREAKFAST AT TIFFANY'S, by Truman Capote. (Random House.)

FAMOUS BIRTHDAYS OF 1959

January – February

4 January – John Batchelor, racing driver, businessman and political activist (died 2010)

5 January – David Eastwood, English historian and academic

7 January – Angela Smith, British Labour Co-operative politician and MP for Basildon

12 January – Simon Tolkien, novelist

16 January – Sade Adu, Nigerian-born British singer-songwriter and record producer

29 January – Frank Key, writer (died 2019)

30 January – Alex Hyde-White, English actor

3 February – Lol Tolhurst, cofounder and drummer/keyboardist of rock band The Cure

4 February – John Wraw, Anglican prelate (died 2017)

6 February – Martyn Quayle, politician (died 2016)

7 February – Mick McCarthy, football player and manager

11 February – Deborah Meaden, businesswoman

15 February - Adam Boulton, English journalist

Ali Campbell, English singer-songwriter and guitarist

Martin Rowson, English author and illustrator

17 February – Dave Courtney, gangster, author and actor (died 2023)

18 February - Jayne Atkinson, English-born actress

David Parker, swimmer (died 2010)

23 February – Richard Dodds, British field hockey player

27 February – Simon Critchley, British philosopher

March – April

1 March – Nick Griffin, British politician, chairman of the British National Party (BNP)

9 March – Mark Carwardine, British zoologist

15 March – Ben Okri, Nigerian-born poet and novelist

19 March – Terry Hall, British singer (died 2022)

20 March

Steve McFadden, British actor

Peter Truscott, Baron Truscott, Labour politician and peer

21 March – Colin Jones, Welsh boxer

29 March – Richard Cousins, English businessman (died 2017)

30 March – Andrew Bailey, English banker

4 April – Gordon Dunne, Northern Irish politician (died 2021)

5 April – Ian Pearson, British Labour politician and MP for Dudley South

7 April – Nigel Walker, footballer (died 2014)

9 April – Bernard Jenkin, politician

11 April – John Myers, radio executive (died 2019)

14 April – Ali Brownlee, radio sports broadcaster (died 2016)

15 April – Emma Thompson, English actress, comedian and screenwriter

16 April

Yvonne Carter, general practitioner and academic (died 2009)

Alison Ramsay, Scottish field hockey player

17 April

Imogen Bain, actress (died 2014)

Sean Bean, actor

Peter Doig, British painter

19 April – Jane Campbell, Baroness Campbell of Surbiton, disability rights campaigner

21 April – Robert Smith, gothic rock singer-songwriter (The Cure)

24 April – Paula Yates, television presenter (died 2000)

25 April – Adrian Sanders, British Liberal Democrat politician and MP for Torbay

27 April – Sheena Easton, Scottish singer

May – June

3 May – Ben Elton, English comedian and writer

4 May – Dick Bradsell, bartender (died 2016)

5 May – Ian McCulloch, English rock singer-songwriter (Echo & the Bunnymen)

8 May – Kevin McCloud, television presenter

12 May

Mark Davies, Roman Catholic bishop of Shrewsbury

Deborah Warner, stage director and producer

13 May – Peter Longbottom, cyclist (died 1998)

15 May – Andrew Eldritch, né Taylor, English gothic rock singer-songwriter (The Sisters of Mercy)

16 May – Tracy Hyde, English actress and model

17 May – Richard Barrons, English general

18 May

Graham Dilley, cricketer (died 2011)

Rupert Soames, businessman

20 May – Gregory Gray, Northern Irish singer-songwriter (died 2019)

22 May

Graham Fellows, English comedy performer

Morrissey, English alternative rock singer-songwriter

Jon Sopel, journalist and television presenter

23 May – Bob Mortimer, English comedian and actor

24 May – Sharon Peacock, microbiologist

27 May – Gerard Kelly, Scottish actor (died 2010)

28 May

Bernardine Evaristo, author and academic

John Morgan, writer and etiquette expert (died 2000)

29 May

Rupert Everett, English actor[40]

Adrian Paul, English-born actor

Tessa Tennant, English green investment campaigner (died 2018)

30 May – David Thomas, cricketer (died 2012)

1 June

Martin Brundle, English Formula One motor racing driver

John Pullinger, English statistician and librarian

Peter Skinner, English Labour politician and MEP for South East England

6 June – Lindsay Posner, English theatre director and manager

11 June – Hugh Laurie, English actor, comedian and writer

19 June

Ray Deakin, footballer (died 2008)

Sophie Grigson, English cookery writer and celebrity chef

21 June – John Baron, English Conservative politician and MP for Billericay

24 June – Andy McCluskey, musician and songwriter (OMD)

26 June – Lucy Kellaway, English columnist at the Financial Times and teacher

27 June – Clint Boon, English rock keyboardist (Inspiral Carpets) and DJ

28 June – Sally Morgan, Baroness Morgan of Huyton, English Labour politician and educationalist

29 June – Richard Vranch, English comedian, actor and television panel show participant

30 June – Jane Gregory, Olympic equestrian (died 2011)

July – August

3 July

Julie Burchill, journalist

Graham Roberts, footballer and manager

4 July – Jan Brittin, cricketer (died 2017)

8 July – Pauline Quirke, actress

11 July – Steve Whatley, actor and television presenter (died 2005)

13 July – Richard Leman, field hockey player

15 July – Charles Farr, civil servant (died 2019)

16 July – James MacMillan, composer and conductor

18 July – Jonathan Dove, operatic composer

31 July – Kim Newman, journalist, film critic and fiction writer

1 August

Joe Elliott, rock singer (Def Leppard)

Desmond Noonan, gangster (died 2005)

5 August – Pete Burns, pop singer (died 2016)

19 August – Russell Foster, neuroscientist

20 August – Andrew Pelling, Conservative politician and MP for Croydon Central

24 August – Meg Munn, Labour Co-operative politician and MP for Sheffield Heeley

27 August – Jeanette Winterson, novelist

28 August – John Yems, football manager

29 August – Stephen Wolfram, scientist

September – October

5 September – Michael Lord-Castle, business person

8 September – Judy Murray, tennis coach

11 September – Colin Butts, novelist and screenwriter (died 2018)

12 September

Mike Barrett, footballer (died 1984)

Julia Samuel, psychotherapist

13 September – Andy Gray, Scottish actor (died 2021)

18 September

Ian Arkwright, English footballer

Lucy Birley, model, photographer and socialite (died 2018)

20 September – Kevin Stonehouse, footballer (died 2019)

21 September – Corinne Drewery, singer-songwriter and fashion designer

23 September

Frank Cottrell-Boyce, writer

Karen Pierce, British diplomat

24 September – Drummie Zeb, reggae musician (died 2022)

28 September – Paul 'Trouble' Anderson, DJ (died 2018)

4 October – Chris Lowe, synth-pop singer-songwriter

7 October – Simon Cowell, English music producer and television talent show judge

10 October

Mark Johnston, Scottish-born racehorse trainer

Kirsty MacColl, British singer-songwriter (died 2000)

15 October

Sarah, Duchess of York

Tibor Fischer, British fiction writer

Andy Holmes, rower (died 2010)

16 October

Gary Kemp, English pop artist (Spandau Ballet)

John Whittingdale, British Conservative politician and MP for Maldon and Chelmsford East

20 October – Niamh Cusack, Irish-born actress

21 October – Cleveland Watkiss, jazz vocalist

24 October – Ruth Perednik, English-Israeli psychologist and academic

27 October – Liz Howe, ecologist (died 2019)

November – December

1 November – Susanna Clarke, British writer

2 November

Kevin Ashman, English quiz player

Peter Mullan, Scottish actor

9 November

Andy Kershaw, British music broadcaster

Frances O'Grady, British trades union leader

13 November – Caroline Goodall, actress

14 November – Paul McGann, British actor

18 November – Jimmy Quinn, Irish footballer and football manager

25 November

Mark Andrews, rower (died 2020)

Charles Kennedy, Scottish Liberal Democrat politician (died 2015)

26 November – Dai Davies Welsh politician and independent MP

30 November – Lorraine Kelly, Scottish presenter and journalist

1 December – Billy Childish, English painter, writer and musician

2 December – Gwyneth Strong, British actress

5 December – Robbie France, drummer (died 2012)

6 December – Stephen Hepburn, British Labour MP for Jarrow

10 December – Kevin Ash, journalist and author (d. 2013)

11 December – Phil Woolas, disgraced Labour MP

12 December – Jasper Conran, English designer

28 December – Andy McNab, British soldier turned novelist

29 November – Richard Borcherds, mathematician

30 December – Tracey Ullman, English comedian, actress, singer, dancer, screenwriter and author

Unknown dates

Dilly Braimoh, African-British television presenter and producer

Amanda Craig, British novelist

Edith Hall, classicist

Mick Hume, British journalist and organiser of the Revolutionary Communist Party

Mick Manning, British children's author and illustrator

Jasper Morrison, English product and furniture designer

DEATHS OF THE YEAR

14 January – G. D. H. Cole, political and economic theorist, historian and detective fiction writer (born 1889)

22 January – Mike Hawthorn, English race car driver (car crash) (born 1929)

15 February – Sir Owens Willans Richardson, British physicist, Nobel Prize laureate (born 1879)

21 February – Kathleen Freeman, classical scholar (born 1897)

26 February – Princess Alexandra, 2nd Duchess of Fife (Princess Arthur of Connaught), member of the royal family (born 1891)

25 April – Janet Philip, academic administrator (born 1876)

11 June – Gordon Selwyn, educator and Anglican priest (born 1885)

11 July – Charlie Parker, English cricketer (born 1882)

5 August – Edgar A. Guest, English poet (born 1881)

19 August

Jacob Epstein, an American-born British sculptor (born 1880)

Claude Grahame-White, English aviator (born 1879)

6 September – Kay Kendall, English actress (born 1926) (leukaemia)

21 September – Agnes Nicholls, operatic soprano (born 1877)

25 September

Gerard Hoffnung, German-born humourist (born 1925)

Vera Laughton Mathews, naval officer (born 1888)

15 November – Charles Thomson Rees Wilson, Scottish physicist, Nobel Prize laureate (born 1869)

26 November – Albert Ketèlbey, pianist, conductor and composer (born 1875)

14 December – Stanley Spencer, painter (born 1891)

TELEVISION BBC AND SOUND

RADIO TIMES

PRICE FOURPENCE

A HAPPY
NEW YEAR!

JANUARY 1ST 1959 BBC1 TELEVISION SCHEDULE

11:15 am Waltzes from Vienna

Part of the New Year's Day Concert by the Vienna Philharmonic Orchestra.

Conducted in the traditional Strauss' manner by Willy Boskovsky, Leader of the Orchestra.

(Broadcast by courtesy of the Austrian Television Service) (to 12.15)

Contributors: Musicians: The Vienna Philharmonic Orchestra. Conductor: Willy Boskovsky

13:15 Beunydd

Bwrw golwg dros bynciau'r dydd mewn sgwrs a ffilm - a chyfle i gwrdd a rhai sy'n amlwg yn y newyddion.

(Wenvoe, Blaen-Plwyf, Holme Moss, and Sutton Coldfield only) (to 13.30)

14:30 Watch with Mother: Rag, Tag, and Bobtail

14:45 Mainly for Women: Family Affairs: Acting for Young People.

What can young people get out of acting? How can they get help and advice in mounting plays?

Jean Metcalfe interviews John Allen, and questions Peter Carpenter and Frances Mackenzie about the activities of the British Drama League. Members of the Junior Drama League present a play.

3.15 Cookery Club

Marguerite Patten introduces the winner of the competition for yeast cakes and demonstrates her recipe. (to 15.30)

Contributors: Interviewer (Family Affairs: Acting for Young People): Jean Metcalfe Interviewee (Family Affairs: Acting for Young People)

17:00 Children's Television presents: Blue Peter

Toys, model railways games, stories, cartoons. A weekly programme for younger viewers with Christopher Trace and Leila Williams.

Contributors: Presenter: Christopher Trace Presenter: Leila Williams Producer: John Hunter Blair

17:15 Children's Television: Whirlybirds: Sky Hook

A coastguard on his lonely cliff patrol discovers two young people stranded on the rocks below. Chuck Martin and P.T. Moore are summoned to the rescue-but to land on the rocks is impossible, and the tide advances rapidly. There's just one chance - and Chuck and P.T. decide to take it!

Contributors: P.T. Moore: Craig Hill, Chuck Martin: Kenneth Tobey

17:40 Children's Television: Junior Sportsview

Peter Dimmock introduces Junior Sportsview Today's edition includes: 'Improve Your Swimming' with Olympic Gold Medallist Judy Grinham, and films and reports from the world of sport. Contributors: Presenter: Peter Dimmock Swimmer (Improve Your Swimming): Judy Grinham Presented by: Tom Millett Editor: Ronnie Noble

18:00 On transmitters serving the areas: 6.10 News for Scotland,

Northern Ireland, and the English Regions

News from Wales: 6.15-6.20

18:20 The Burns and Allen Show: The Magic Act Starring George Burns and Gracie Allen in the film The Magic Act

Contributors: Himself: George Burns Herself: Gracie Allen

18:45 Tonight Look around with Cliff Michelmore. Sport - Music - People Cinema - Theatre - Argument

with Derek Hart, Geoffrey Johnson Smith, Macdonald Hastings and this week, Cy Grant and Noel Harrison. Contributors: Presenter: Cliff Michelmore Reporter: Derek Hart Reporter: Geoffrey Johnson Smith Reporter: Macdonald Hastings Singer/guitarist: Cy Grant Singer/guitarist: Noel Harrison Producer: Donald Baverstock

19:25 News Summary

19:30 Vera Lynn Sings

in which Vera meets some old friends Rawicz and Landauer. Some pages of her record album are turned by The Lynnettes. Also with her are The Leslie Roberts Silhouettes and Guest Artists The Hedley Ward Trio, Bobby Watson.

20:15 Time Out of Mind

A play by Geoffrey Trease. From the BBC's North of England studios (Ann Firbank appears by permission of Ealing MGM Artists, Ltd.)

Contributors: Writer: Geoffrey Trease Producer: Desmond Davis Designer: Keith Featherstone

21:30 The Men Behind the Music

Alan Jay Lerner and Frederick Loewe present the music of 'My Fair Lady', and

'Brigadoon' and introduce the European premiere of the score of MGM's latest musical film 'Gigi'. The programme was devised and produced by Charles R. Rogers with Sidney Torch and his Orchestra, Stephanie Voss, Edith Stevenson, Barry Sinclair, and Alan Edwards. (Stephanie Voss appears by permission of Associated Television Limited)

22:00: News

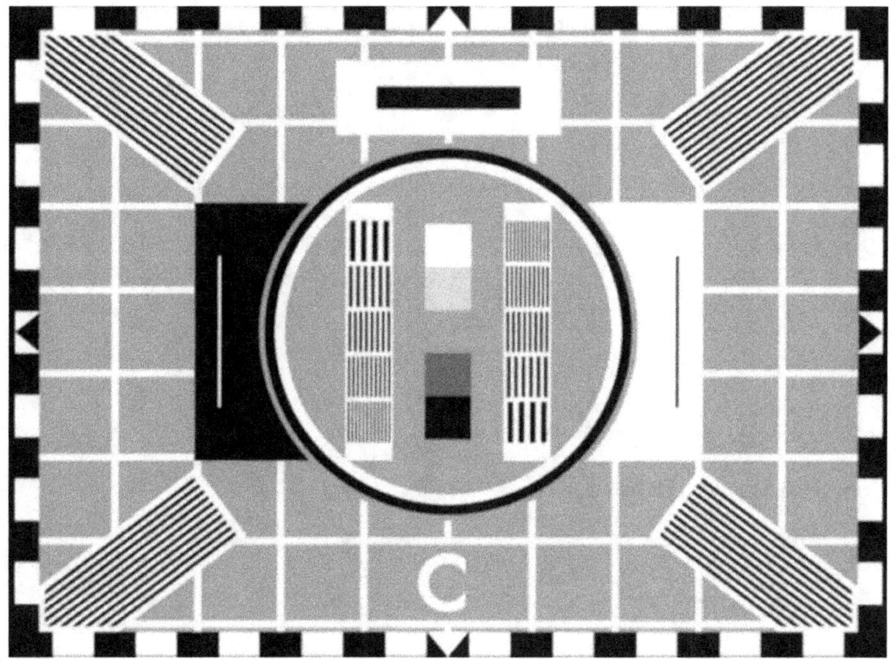

How much did things cost in 1959?

These are some prices of a few items in 1959.

1959 price Inflation adjusted

Pint of beer (bottled) 1s 10d £1.60

20 cigarettes 3s 11d £3.50

Loaf of bread (white, unwrapped) 11d 81p

Loose leaf tea 4oz 1s 8d £1.50

Sugar 1lb 8d 59p

Pint of milk 8d 59p

Butter ½lb 2s 2d £1.90

Cheddar cheese 1lb 3s 5d £3

Margarine 1lb 1s 8½d £1.50

Lard 1lb 1s 4½d £1.20

Eggs 1 dozen 2s 3½d £2

Potatoes lb 3½d 26p

Cabbages lb 5½d 40p

Onions lb 6d 44p

Eating apples lb 1s 88p

Oranges lb 1s 88p

Ground coffee 8oz 3s 9d £3.30

Cocoa lb 4s 6d £4

Coal - 1cwt 7s 6d £6.60

Ekco 17" television 65 guineas £1,200

Cossor 1300T transistor radio 18½ guineas £340

Qualcast Panther push lawn mower £8 12s 6d £150

The Daily Mirror newspaper 2½d 18p

Average house price £2,124 £37,000

Ford Anglia car £589 £10,000

Candy Bi-Matic Twin Tub washing machine 85 guineas £1,600

Electric vacuum cleaner 7 guineas £130

Bic Crystal ballpoint pen 1s 88p

Prices are in pounds, shillings and pence.

Some shops priced more expensive items in guineas. A guinea is one pound and one shilling or £1.05.

The inflation-adjusted prices are based on the Consumer Price Index (CPI).

In those days, the average weekly wage was £9.25, and the average house was worth £2,064.

Here we list some of the things you could have got for your money back then.

A GALLON of petrol cost four shillings and sixpence - that's 22p in today's money.

A PACKET of cigarettes cost 18p.

A POUND of butter was 18p, a loaf was 4p, a pint of milk 3p and six eggs just 8p.

FOR £1, you could have bought 15 pints of beer, 14 fish suppers or gone to the cinema 10 times.

In 1955 only eight per cent of people owned their own homes compared to nearly 70 per cent today.

In the same year, the government forked out £1.2billion to electrify the rail network - a record amount in today's money.

In 1959, the United Kingdom's currency system was based on the pound sterling (£), which was further divided into shillings and pence. This system was commonly referred to as "pounds, shillings, and pence" or "LSD." Here's a breakdown of the currency system in the UK in 1959:

British Currency Explained (For those who you who have forgotten)

1. Pound (£): The pound was the basic unit of currency and represented the highest denomination. It was often abbreviated as "£." There were 20 shillings in one pound.

2. Shilling (s): The shilling, denoted by the symbol " s, " was a subdivision of the pound. Twelve pence made one shilling, so twenty shillings (20 shillings x 12 pence) made one pound.

3. Penny (d): The penny was the smallest denomination and was denoted by the symbol "d." There were 12 pennies in one shilling.

So, the hierarchical breakdown was as follows:

- 1 Pound (£) = 20 Shillings (s)

- 1 Shilling (s) = 12 Pence (d)

In practical terms, prices and wages were often quoted in pounds, shillings, and pence. For example, something might cost £1 5s 6d, which meant 1 pound, 5 shillings, and 6 pence. To convert this into decimal currency, you would add up the values: 1 pound + (5 shillings / 20) + (6 pence / 240).

1959 FIRST DIVISION FOOTBALL TABLE

The Football League - Season 1958–59

Champions - Wolverhampton Wanderers

The 1958–59 season was the 60th completed season of The Football League.

This season saw the introduction of the Fourth Division.

Beginning with the 1894–95 season, clubs finishing level on points were separated according to goal average (goals scored divided by goals conceded), or more properly, goal ratio. The goal average system was eventually scrapped beginning with the 1976–77 season.

From this season, the bottom four teams of the Fourth Division were required to apply for re-election.[2]

Champions: Wolverhampton Wanderers (3rd English title)

Relegated: Aston Villa & Portsmouth

European Cup: Wolverhampton Wanderers

Matches played 462

Goals scored 1,692 (3.66 per match)

Top goalscorer Jimmy Greaves (33 goals)

Biggest home win: Wolverhampton Wanderers 7–0 Portsmouth (27 December 1958)

Biggest away win Birmingham City 0–6 West Bromwich Albion (3 September 1958)

Nottingham Forest 1–7 Birmingham City (7 March 1959)

Highest scoring Tottenham Hotspur 10–4 Everton (11 October 1958)

Diary of the Season

August 1958: The Football League season begins with the new national Third and Fourth divisions that have been created from the old Third Division North and Third Division South.

30 August 1958: The Football Association snub Manchester United's wish to participate in the 1958–59 European Cup.

September 1958: Manchester United pay a national record fee of £45,000 for Sheffield Wednesday inside-forward Albert Quixall.

12 November 1958: Wolverhampton Wanderers play their first European Cup game, drawing 2–2 at home to Schalke 04 in the first round first leg.

18 November 1958: Wolverhampton Wanderers lose 2–1 to Schalke 04 in the European Cup first round second leg in West Germany, ending their hopes of being the first team other than Real Madrid (winners of the first three competitions) to win the European Cup.

4 April 1959: Jeff Hall, 29, right-back for Birmingham City and England, dies from polio, prompting widespread takeup of the polio vaccine.

2 May 1959: Nottingham Forest defeat Luton Town 2–1 in the 1959 FA Cup Final.

Notable debutants: 8 September 1958: Bobby Moore, 17-year-old wing-half, makes his debut for West Ham United against Manchester United in the First Division. Notable retirements: May 1959: Billy Wright, 35, Wolverhampton Wanderers and England captain, after more than 500 appearances for his club and a record 105 for his country.

Pos	Team	Pld	W	D	L	GF	GA	GAv.	Pts
1	*Wolverhampton Wanderers (C)*	42	28	5	9	110	49	2.245	**61**
2	*Manchester United*	42	24	7	11	103	66	1.561	**55**
3	*Arsenal*	42	21	8	13	88	68	1.294	**50**
4	*Bolton Wanderers*	42	20	10	12	79	66	1.197	**50**
5	*West Bromwich Albion*	42	18	13	11	88	68	1.294	49
6	*West Ham United*	42	21	6	15	85	70	1.214	48
7	*Burnley*	42	19	10	13	81	70	1.157	48
8	*Blackpool*	42	18	11	13	66	49	1.347	47
9	*Birmingham City*	42	20	6	16	84	68	1.235	46
10	*Blackburn Rovers*	42	17	10	15	76	70	1.086	44
11	*Newcastle United*	42	17	7	18	80	80	1.000	41
12	*Preston North End*	42	17	7	18	70	77	0.909	41
13	*Nottingham Forest*	42	17	6	19	71	74	0.959	40
14	*Chelsea*	42	18	4	20	77	98	0.786	40
15	*Leeds United*	42	15	9	18	57	74	0.770	39

16	Everton	42	17	4	21	71	87	0.816	38
17	Luton Town	42	12	13	17	68	71	0.958	37
18	Tottenham Hotspur	42	13	10	19	85	95	0.895	36
19	Leicester City	42	11	10	21	67	98	0.684	32
20	Manchester City	42	11	9	22	64	95	0.674	31
21	Aston Villa (R)	42	11	8	23	58	87	0.667	30
22	Portsmouth (R)	42	6	9	27	64	112	0.571	21

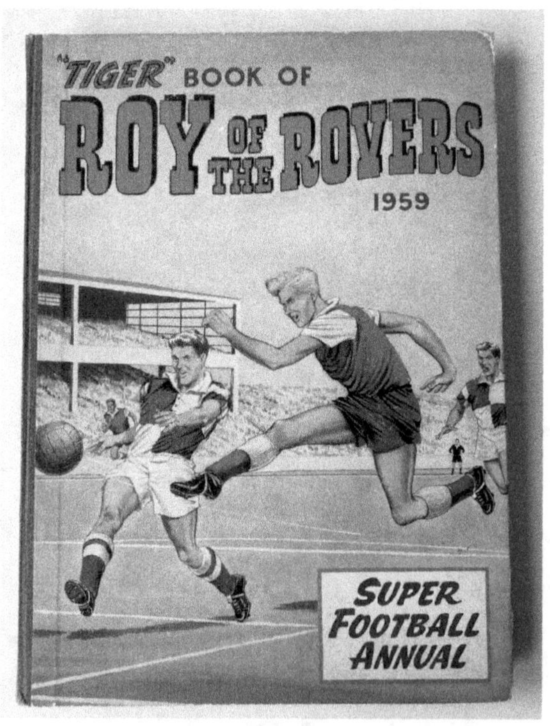

THE SPACE RACE
WHAT EXACTLY WERE THOSE CRAZY SCIENTISTS UP TO IN 1959?

THE SPACE RACE AND TECHNOLOGY

In May, two monkeys became the first monkeys to survive a space flight. Able, a rhesus monkey, and Baker, a squirrel monkey, were launched into space from Cape Canaveral by the United States Army on a Jupiter am-18 rocket. They reached an altitude of about 360 miles, and their flight lasted about 15 minutes in total. They successfully returned to earth, splashing down about 1,500 miles away from the launch site, near Puerto Rico in the Atlantic Ocean and were recovered. Able and Baker were not the first animals to survive space flight as the United States launched fruit flies that were successfully recovered in 1947, and the soviet union had several dogs that were recovered from sub-orbital flight in the early 1950s.

Miss Baker and Miss Able were the first us animals to successfully fly to and return from space alive. Miss Baker was chosen during a training program among 25 other animals at the Naval School of Aviation Medicine. While she flew into space in her own space flight capsule, Miss Baker was monitored by electrodes to keep an eye on her physiological state. The primates made their journey into space on May 28, in a Huntsville-built Jupiter rocket. In total, the monkeys travelled to an altitude of more than 300 miles, and more than 1,700 ground miles. They also travelled at speeds of more than 10,000 mph. When the monkeys returned to earth, they were unharmed and seemed in good spirits. However, Miss Able unfortunately passed away on an operating table just four days after her return to Earth, during an operation to remove one of her electrodes. Miss Baker went to live at the Naval Aerospace Medical Center in Pensacola, Florida. She was even given a companion, big George, to keep her company. Both monkeys remained at the centre until 1971, when they were moved to the U S. Space and Rocket

Centre in Huntsville, Alabama.

Miss Baker lived for 27 years, which is the oldest age a squirrel monkey has reportedly lived. She died on November 29, 1984, after a very busy post-space travel life of TV appearances and public visits.

United States - pioneer 4 spacecraft

NASA launched the Pioneer 4 spacecraft on March 3. Pioneer 4 was the first American spacecraft to exit the orbit of Earth, though the soviet union had already achieved the same feat in January with their Luna 1 spacecraft. Pioneer 4 travelled within 37,000 miles of the moon and had sensors on board that would allow it to transmit photos of the lunar surface. Unfortunately, its sensors were not activated as it never came close enough to the moon to trigger them due to a trajectory error. The signal from Pioneer 4 was lost after 82 hours in space and 655,000 miles of travel, a record at the time for the farthest a man-made object had travelled through space.

Ussr - the Luna 2 spacecraft crashes into the moon

the soviet union crashed the Luna 2 spacecraft into the moon, making it the first man-made object to reach the moon's surface. The Luna 2 (Lunik 2) was launched on September 12th, and after over thirty hours of flight, it crashed into the surface of the moon on September 14th. The spacecraft carried soviet pennants and several scientific instruments like a Geiger counter to measure radiation and a magnetometer to measure magnetic fields. It ceased operation after impacting the moon in the Palus Putredinus region. This was one of the first major events in the space race between the United States and the soviet union. The United States did not successfully land a spacecraft on the moon under the Ranger 4 in 1962.

U. S. - mercury seven the first us astronauts.

NASA introduced the world to America's first astronauts, including John H. Glenn Jr. and Alan Shepard Jr.

NASA introduced the first group of astronauts, known as the Mercury Seven, in April. The astronauts were Alan Shepard, John Glenn, Walter Schirra, Donald Slayton, Virgil "Gus" Grissom, l. Gordon Cooper, and m. Scott Carpenter. The group consisted of military aviators, 3 from the Navy, 3 from the Air Force, and

1 from the Marine Corps. The astronauts took part in the United States' first human space flight program, Project Mercury. Many of the men would also go on to take part in future NASA projects such as the Gemini program and the Apollo program. Some notable achievements by the Mercury Seven included Alan Shepard becoming the first American in space and John Glenn becoming the first American to orbit the Earth.

Technology

- Boeing 707 jet airliner comes into service cutting 8 hours from transatlantic flight

- first pictures of Earth from space taken by explorer 6

- IBM shipped the transistor-based IBM 1401 mainframe.

- Full-size hovercraft, the sr-n1 by sir Christopher Cockerell tested for the first time on June 11th at Cowes on the Isle of Wight

- xerox launches the first commercial copier

- us launches first weather station in space

- the first section of the M1 motorway from London to Birmingham opens

- De Beers manufactures a synthetic diamond

- Qantas introduced the Boeing 707 on its Sydney-San Francisco route, the first transpacific service flown by jet.

- Inventions invented by inventors and country (or attributed to first use)

- microchip USA by Jack Kilby

- etch a sketch was invented in France by Arthur Grandjean

- computer modem USA

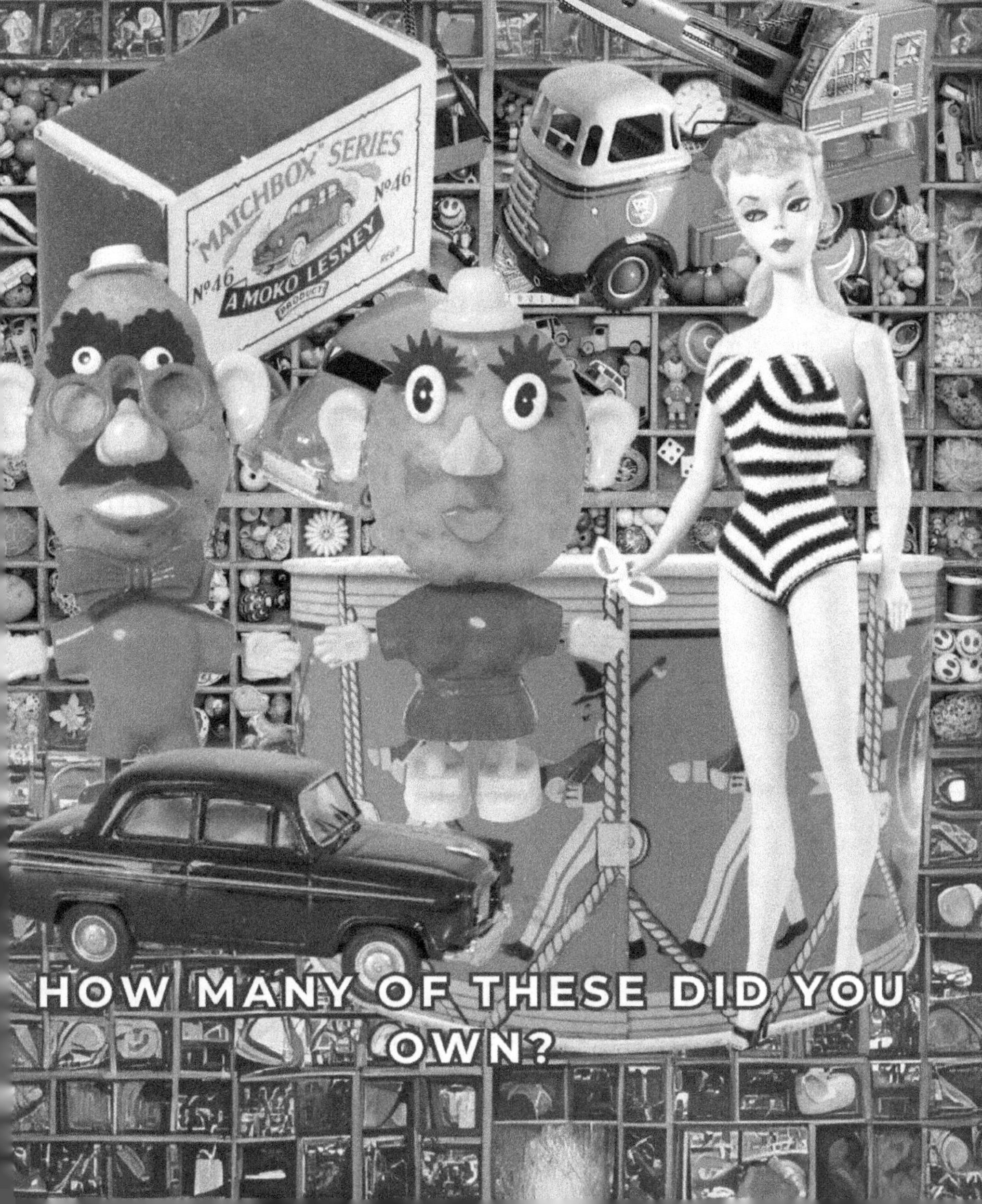
POPULAR TOYS OF 1959
"MATCHBOX" SERIES
No 46
No 46
A MOKO LESNEY
PRODUCT
HOW MANY OF THESE DID YOU OWN?

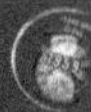

POPULAR TOYS OF 1959

Barbie

The most popular topy for girls in 1959, was the Barbie doll. Original estimated retail price: $3, Ruth Handler created the first Barbie as a 3D alternative to the paper dolls her daughter used to play with. Barbie remains the most iconic doll of all time. Naturally, that meteoric success came with its share of criticism, namely from feminists who thought Barbie's curvy physique and penchant for teen fashion set a bad example for young girls. Agreeing to a point, toy company Mattel went to great lengths over the years to establish Barbie as a symbol of inclusion and female empowerment, giving her varying ethnicities, careers, and styles. Barbie is one of the most popular toys ever designed, Barbie changed the game for doll manufacturers and gave little girls a chance to experiment with fashion.

Some other popular toys from 1959:

1. Scalextric: Introduced in the late 1950s, Scalextric was a popular slot car racing game that quickly became a classic toy.

2. Hornby Dublo Trains: Hornby Dublo, a model railway system, was widely enjoyed by children and enthusiasts. It offered realistic train sets and accessories.

3. Muffin the Mule Puppet: Based on the popular children's television character Muffin the Mule, puppet versions of Muffin were available, and they became sought-after toys.

4. Airfix Model Kits: Airfix model kits, particularly those of aeroplanes, ships, and military vehicles, gained popularity. These kits allowed children to build and paint detailed scale models.

5. Fuzzy Felt: Fuzzy felt sets, featuring felt pieces that could be arranged on a fuzzy board to create scenes and pictures, were popular educational toys.

6. Teddy Bears: Teddy bears continued to be a beloved toy. Traditional brands like Steiff and Merrythought produced teddy bears that were cherished by children.

7. Dinky Toys: Dinky Toys, produced by Meccano Ltd., were die-cast miniature vehicles, including cars, trucks, and other vehicles. Many children collected and played with them.

8. Dolls and Dollhouses: Dolls, particularly those with realistic features and accessories, remained popular. Dollhouses and miniature furniture sets were also in demand.

These are just a few examples of the toys that were popular in the UK in 1959. Keep in mind that the availability and popularity of toys can vary based on individual preferences and regional trends.

TOP THREE POPULAR CARS OF 1959

1. THE MINI

Few cars can claim the level of importance and iconic status that the original Mini achieved, establishing a blueprint for small cars that persists to this day. Featuring a transversely mounted engine situated over the front wheels and a gearbox sharing the same oil, the Mini presented a compact design that optimized cabin space within its modest 3054 mm (120in) overall length. Its lightweight construction not only contributed to fuel efficiency but also ensured agile handling, with the promise of enhanced performance delivered later by the Cooper models.

The genesis of the Mini, like many groundbreaking designs, traces back to the bold vision of one man—Alec Issigonis, who had previously conceptualized the Morris Minor. It is crucial to acknowledge that the Mini's creation was also influenced by the strong aversion of British Motor Corporation boss Leonard Lord toward 'bubble' microcars. Seeking an alternative to these vehicles that gained popularity amid the fuel shortages resulting from the 1956 Suez Crisis, Lord's vision materialized into a car that endured in production for an impressive 41 years, boasting a production tally of 5.4 million units.

An Austin de luxe saloon was tested by the British magazine The Motor in 1959. It had a top speed of 72.4 mph (116.5 km/h) and could accelerate from 0–60 mph

(97 km/h) in 27.1 seconds. A fuel consumption of 43.5 mpg-imp (6.49 L/100 km; 36.2 mpg-US) was recorded. The car cost £496.

2. THE TRIUMPH HERALD

Distinguished by Michelotti's sleek design, the Triumph Herald stood out from competitors like the Ford Anglia and Mini. Despite its captivating exterior, the Herald concealed a separate chassis born out of necessity and constrained by a limited budget. Nevertheless, this did not hinder the Herald from attracting a substantial customer base, with a total of 951,289 units sold across all variants by the time production ceased in 1971. Additionally, 51,000 Vitesse models, equipped with a six-cylinder engine, contributed to this success.

The initial offering in the Herald lineup was the Coupe, swiftly followed by the 4-door and convertible versions a couple of weeks later. In 1961, an estate model with an expanded 1200 engine joined the range. The year 1967 witnessed the introduction of the restyled 13/60, featuring a larger 1.3-litre motor. All variants retained the original transverse leaf rear spring suspension, a characteristic that could catch the unwary. Despite this potential drawback, the Herald demonstrated its prowess as a rally car, securing works entries and clinching a class victory in the 1960 RAC Rally.

It brought in younger buyers to the company, helped by its £702 price. A Mini was just £496, but the Herald was viewed as a more premium choice, and Ford worked out that BMC was losing money on every Mini it sold to begin with. Initially, Triumph sold the Herald as a saloon or coupé.

3. THE FORD ANGLIA

The introduction of the 105E Anglia by Ford in 1959 marked a revolutionary departure from the previous generation. Dispensing with the plump, rounded aesthetics, the 105E Anglia embraced razor-sharp lines, fins, and a distinctive reverse-angle back window—an infusion of the American dream into a compact size.

True to the Ford legacy, the Anglia swiftly became a favourite in the tuning world, owing to its spirited 997cc four-cylinder engine and nimble handling. It held its ground against the Mini on both track and rally stages, significantly enhancing its reputation and achieving sales surpassing 1 million units before gracefully stepping aside in 1967 to make room for the Escort. In more recent times, the Anglia has garnered renewed attention as a prominent star in the Harry Potter movies.

The cost of the car? £589 in 1959. Dig deep!

MOTORWAYS

The first section of the M1 motorway between junction 5 (Watford) and junction 18 (Crick/Rugby), opened on 2nd November 1959, together with the motorway's two spurs, the M10 (from junction 7 to south of St Albans originally connecting to the A1) and the M45 (from junction 17 to the A45 and Coventry).

It was not the first, though. Britain's first motorway, the Preston by-pass, opened in 1958. Designed by Lancashire County Council under civil engineer Sir James Drake – regarded as the pioneer of the UK motorway network – it's now part of the M6. The next 10 years saw the UK's network expand as hundreds of miles of motorway were built.

Initially, the M1 witnessed a notable uptick in breakdowns among the average British small cars soon after its inauguration. These vehicles, not initially designed for extended periods of cruising at 70mph, frequently succumbed to issues such as overheating, tyre blowouts, or fan belt failures when subjected to sustained high speeds. In contrast, larger luxury cars like Jaguars, Rovers, Volvos, Bentleys, and Rolls Royce exhibited greater resilience, managing to endure the rigours of high-speed travel. Manufacturers eventually responded to the challenges posed by sustained high speeds, implementing changes to enhance the small cars' capability to withstand such conditions. It took several years of development before British small cars could navigate the M1 and subsequent motorways comfortably.

YOU KNOW YOU
ARE OLD WHEN...

YOU KNOW YOU ARE OLD WHEN... (A LIST OF FIFTY ITEMS IN LARGE PRINT FORMAT)

1. You know you are old when you've been there and done that but don't remember what *that* was.

2. You know you are old when you stop growing at both ends and start growing in the middle.

3. You know you are old when people tell you how good you look.

4. You know you are old when almost everything hurts, and what doesn't hurt doesn't work.

5. You know you are old when the candles cost more than the cake.

6. You know you are old when you hear your favourite songs in an elevator.

7. You know you're old when your doctor tells you to slow down, not the police.

8. You know you are old when you write a note to yourself reminding you not to take a sleeping pill and a laxative on the same night.

9. You know you are old when people no longer view you as a hypochondriac.

10. You know you are 100 years old when you see expensive antiques, and you remember one just like it that you threw away.

11. You ask the garage to check why your car is costing so little to run.

12. You wonder how you could be over the hill when you don't even remember

being on top of it.

13. The gleam in your eyes is from the sun hitting your bifocals.

14. You feel like the morning after, and you haven't been anywhere.

15. Your little black book contains only names that end in M.D.

16. Your children begin to look middle-aged.

17. You finally reach the top of the ladder and find it leaning against the wrong wall.

18. You look forward to a dull evening.

19. Your favourite part of the newspaper is "20 Years Ago Today."

20. You turn out the lights for economic rather than romantic reasons.

21. You sit in a rocking chair and can't get it going.

22. Your knees buckle, and your belt won't.

23. Your back goes out more than you do.

24. The little old grey-haired lady you helped across the street is your wife.

25. You sink your teeth into a steak, and they stay there.

26. You have too much room in the house and not enough in the medicine cabinet.

27. You know all the answers, but nobody asks you the questions.

28. You're asleep, but others worry that you're dead.

29. You are proud of your lawn mower.

30. Your arms are almost too short to read the newspaper.

31. You no longer think of speed limits as a challenge.

32. Neighbours borrow your tools.

33. People call at 9 p.m. and ask, "Did I wake you?"

34. The end of your tie doesn't come anywhere near the top of your pants.

35. You know what the word "equity" means.

36. Your ears are hairier than your head.

37. You get into a heated argument about pension plans.

38. The bottle of shampoo has been in the shower for so long that you are starting to think it might be a mystical experience - a loaves-and-fishes thing.

39. You and your teeth don't sleep together.

40. You try to straighten out the wrinkles in your socks and discover you aren't wearing any.

41. At the breakfast table, you hear snap, crackle, pop, and you're not eating cereal.

42. When you wake up looking like your driver's license picture.

43. It takes two tries to get up from the couch.

44. When your idea of a night out is sitting on the patio.

45. When happy hour is a nap.

46. 12. When you step off a curb and look down one more time to make sure the street is still there.

47. 14. It takes longer to rest than it does to get tired.

48. Your memory is shorter, and your complaining lasts longer.

49. You sit in a rocking chair and can't get it going.

50. The pharmacist has become your new best friend.

51. You can't count to fifty without checking.

A LITTLE BIT OF TIME TRAVEL?

The
TWILIGHT
ZONE

Hopefully, this book has made you stop, think – and remember. Doesn't it seem strange that times have changed so much? It's the little things that have changed beyond recognition that we take so much for granted. It's not just the currency – did we really manage to navigate so many pennies in the pound so easily? Were we accustomed to the coal man delivering coal, to there only being three TV channels – and in black and white?

So let's look at it in a little more detail, and above all, remember when times were very different – it is almost like we were brought up in a foreign country!

First of all, in 1959, National Service was still in force (though it did end in 1960), outside toilets were in almost every house, Yout TV set was almost certainly rented, unless you were really posh. Radio Rentals and Rediffusion were the go-to rental firms. It sounds very archaic, but it probably wasn't a bad idea back then – TV sets were notoriously unreliable, suffered from overheating etc.

Do you remember your dad starting a fire in the morning? How about firelighters, soaked in paraffin with that sweet smell that was both enticing and repugnant at the same time?

Then there was school, with the strict teachers and blackboards and long sticks of chalk. Remember also, corporal punishment was perfectly legal, and was so for another twenty-seven years yet, so misbehave at school, and you had the almost certain fate of being caned! Studying was, of course, a completely different kettle of fish. With no internet, your only option for research was visiting a library, or perhaps your parents had a set of handy encyclopaedias bought over the doorstep from the "Encyclopaedia Britannica" man.

If you knew someone who owned a car (and you almost certainly didn't), then there was no need to wear a seatbelt, as it was not a legal requirement until 1983.

You frequently "went out to play", and if you had a bike, it was usually made by Raleigh – do you remember your first bike? Repairing punctures, falling off -though the roads were much quieter then, and cycle helmets were definitely a thing of the future! Did you build a wooden trolley, probably using old pram wheels, and race it down the nearest street?

Did your dad pay the pools man every Friday night, and everyone had to stay completely silent while he marked it from the football results on TV on a Saturday night? Did mum have a thing about polishing the step, and dad was always creosoting the fence? One of your grandparents almost certainly smoked a pipe, with the resulting sweet smell of pipe tobacco that even to this day reminds you of them.

What about letters? You almost always got at least one on your birthday from some distant relative. Or wrote one yourself. It's a forgotten art these days, though. National statistics tell us that more than 20% of children of middle school age these days have never received a letter. Very sad – though, remember, back then, stamps were not self-adhesive and I think we can all remember very well the taste of stamp glue! Yuk!

*"But I don't like to hang up – the operator
is so friendly."*

House telephones were not common at all – and so you were always going to the nearest big red telephone box, which, unlike now, was never very far away, though there was usually a queue, with someone already on the phone completely oblivious to the people waiting outside.

What about holidays? Never abroad – always at home, and how about taking a shower? It was always a bath and was a bit of a ritual rather than commonplace.

So what about the things that we do now that are so normal but in 1959 would have felt like science fiction?

Well, there's the mobile phone, of course, with an instant camera in your pocket, the Internet, watching yesterday's TV today, renting a film instantly, and so on. But there are less obvious things, too, like shopping on a Sunday, taking a shower, using a duvet, using disposable nappies, and charging your toothbrush. Tell someone in 1959 about any of those things – and so many others – then you would have been locked up for sure!

The past is certainly a foreign country, but it's what made us who we are today. I hope you have enjoyed our trip down memory lane, and it has set your cogs turning. Memories, eh? Aren't they just wonderful?

LOOK OUT FOR OUR OTHER TITLES COVERING DIFFERENT YEARS!
YEARS AND YEARS
YEARS AND YEARS
DO YOU REMEMBER THIS?
1958
LIVING DOLL
PEOPLE, MUSIC, FILMS EVENTS IN THE UK FROM THE YEAR YOU WERE BORN!
UK VERSION